More Praise for S

"This book truly distills the esser [...] regret choices you are making today. D [...] g to get to."

CEO of Blucapp

"I have been working with Chris now for several months and can already see that the succession plan that has been eluding us at our company is now within reach with his help and guidance."

~ Ted Goodnow
Founder of Woodmeister Master Builders

"Chris Yonker's sole intention is to help your soul realize its full potential. He'll challenge you to be all you can be and more. Be prepared to read and learn. Even more importantly, get ready to meet your True Self and live the life your soul always intended to live."

~ Thomas J. Shields
"The Optimalogist,"
Optimal Vision Coaching

"I brought Chris on board to help the overall performance of my company. Early on he identified where our weaknesses were and quickly put a plan in place to drive change. He has made a substantial difference and is now considered an important part of our team. My Leadership Team now operates at a higher level than they ever have!"

~ Jim Campanella
President of Lawn Dawg, Inc.

"Someone once said to me, 'Discover a life that requires no escape and you eradicate unhealthy behavior.' Chris has the ability to unpack and bring into focus that which you seek, whether it's peace, professional excellence, forgiveness or personal joy. Spend just 3 minutes with Chris and you will know this truth for yourself."

~ Jeff Photiades
Northwestern Mutual

"This book will help you stop acting like spending more time in one area of your life always has costs in another area—it doesn't have to be this way! You can spend less time at work, more time with family, do more fun activities, and actually be more successful, when you learn how to embrace your Soul Intention in life. You have one life and you have one soul, so stop living like you have countless intentions. Your Soul Intention, when expressed in all you do, breaks down the barriers that have been holding you back all along."

~ Dave Andrews
Author of *The 30-Day Sobriety Solution*

Why *Soul Intention?*

You've always had ambition and *even higher* goals that you want to reach—and you have no intention of dropping out of the game.

After you read this book, you'll have purpose.

Soul Intention: An Executive's Guide to Building a Life by Choice, Not by Chance lays out the key components to achieving true greatness including:

- Why striving harder isn't the key to breaking through to the next level.

- How to optimize your energy so that every aspect of your life gets enough "you."

- What "life balance" means for an executive, and why it's different from the usual advice.

- How to uncover the personal values that keep you aligned with your own "true north."

- What the subconscious barriers are that prevent you from achieving your greatest ambitions, and how rise above them.

- How to break free of the compulsion to fit yourself into a neat little box.

- How to discover and reveal the best version of yourself that leads to unimaginable success.

If you want more from yourself, from your life—and *you want better than what you've seen happen to other people at your level*—then you can have that. You can have it all without sacrificing the rest of your life.

Soul Intention:

An Executive's Guide to Building a Life by Choice, Not by Chance

by Chris Yonker

Chris Yonker
chris@chrisyonker.com
www.chrisyonker.com

Limits of Liability and Disclaimer of Warranty
The author and publisher shall not be liable for your misuse of this material. This book is strictly for informational and educational purposes.

Warning – Disclaimer
The purpose of this book is to educate and entertain. The author and/ or publisher do not guarantee that anyone following these techniques, suggestions, tips, ideas, or strategies will become successful. The author and/ or publisher shall have neither liability nor responsibility to anyone with respect to any loss or damage caused, or alleged to be caused, directly or indirectly by the information contained in this book.

ISBN 978-1-5347-5388-4
Manufactured in the United States of America
First Printing, July 2016

Table of Contents

This book is dedicated to Jolie Yonker
who, more then anyone, encouraged me
to pursue my Soul Intention.

Foreword

Understood.

Have you ever really been understood? Has anyone ever really listened to you? I don't mean just listening to your words. I mean have you ever had the joy of experiencing someone who intently concentrated on understanding your emotions, truly observed you when you communicated (taking into account a complex combination of nonverbal cues), and genuinely listened to what you were saying?

If you have experienced this kind of person, then you know why I used the word *joy*. If you haven't, then you're in for a treat.

Meet Chris Yonker.

Chris and I met a number of years ago when I was President of a medical IT company in the Boston area. He was introduced as an expert communicator, strong motivator, and someone who has a unique ability to influence and elevate one's professional life skills. At that point—some twenty years into my career—I was skeptical of anyone I met in the genre of self-help. *Been there, done that, and never impressed!* was my usual first reaction. And candidly, at that time, I thought I was above it all.

Then Chris spoke his first sentence to me—a question. It was delivered with such sincerity and gentleness that I simply felt compelled to answer. It was like he really wanted to understand the answer, not just hear it so he could start talking again.

The ensuing conversation led to a professional engagement with Chris where he helped me prove that I could take someone, who was outside of the healthcare profession with no sales experience, and turn them into a success with the right training. Chris understood me in such a way that he gave me the information that I could use and benefit from.

And I mean REALLY BENEFIT from.

It also led to a professional and personal relationship that has continuously cemented the importance of first seeking to understand, which is the fifth habit in Stephen Covey's *The 7 Habits of Highly Effective People*: "Seek First to Understand, Then to Be Understood."[1]

If you're anything like me, then you, too, may have been hung up on the latter half of this habit, for far too long. Even though I challenged myself to see the first part of this habit, it wasn't until many years later when I took my first real position heading up a sales team and met my first mentor, that I grasped it and was finally able to comprehend and internalize the value of truly understanding others...for THEIR BENEFIT. When Chris asked me that first question, it was a lightning rod that reminded me of my first mentor and all the professional growth that resulted from it.

Since then, I've seen Chris directly touch and impact the lives of others in many positive ways. Reading this book helped me to recall many of the conversations he and I had, which underscores how deeply Chris pursues understanding the lives that he touches.

Sure, I get it. You're probably saying, *But this is a book...Chris won't be listening to me.* Yet I can tell you firsthand, reading this book is the first step of something much larger. In the pages that follow, you'll learn

---

[1]Stephen Covey, *The 7 Habits of Highly Effective People: Powerful Lessons in Personal Change* (New York: Free Press, 2004), https://www.stephencovey.com/7habits/7habits-habit5.php.

about alignment and how to incorporate your values and start living the life that you want while your business continues on the path to true greatness. Chris furthers the conversation by asking deeper questions at the end of every chapter.

Chris is a force and this book will introduce you to many of the powerful and insightful lessons he offers for your current life, both professionally and personally. I've seen Chris in action, and it is inspiring and humbling both in the same breath.

Today as a CEO, I've learned the value of mentorship and nothing underscores this more than by being a mentor. I've gone on to provide professional mentoring to "up-and-coming" protégés for the past three years. Chris's work continuously reminds me of the importance of a mentor or coach for any level or stage of a career.

If you're a professional that is open to a coach, this book is for you.

And, if you're a professional who is skeptical and closed to a coach or mentor…then this book is DEFINITELY for you.

Enjoy!

Stuart Long
President and CEO at Monarch Medical Technologies
PS: What was that first question he asked me? First, read this book, and then contact Chris and let him ask you directly.

Introduction

Many executives today are driven, often traveling on the edge of burnout. Yet, there are others who live rich, balanced, and fulfilled lives. Why are some energized by the process, sacrificing very little, while others believe they must struggle and sacrifice to have success?

Simply, the latter get caught up spending their time *doing* but rarely see that the root of their problem stems from who they are *being* in the process.

Soul Intention.

As a Neuro-Linguistic Programming (NLP) Practitioner, seventh-degree Master Black Belt, and Executive Performance Coach, I have studied and worked with people in the top 5 percent of their fields. Through my work with these professionals, I have made profound discoveries and found a way to distill these breakthroughs in a way that creates permanent changes in behavior. Most coaches and consultants speak on what to do. I teach you *how* to do it and ask you *why* you want to do it.

> ## *In this book, I challenge you to take control of your destiny and your life—both professionally and personally—and most importantly understand why.*

I share the key elements I've encountered in more than twenty years of study that are needed to achieve success in an enjoyable and authentic way. You will be led through a series of questions that can help unlock your potential and radically alter your thinking as you move forward.

> ## *If you think you know who you are, you will be challenged to become someone else throughout this process.*

My NLP mentor (Wyatt Woodsmall) recounts a story of a friend who approached him for help with a problem. She mentioned that because he specialized in helping people create outcomes she would really appreciate his guidance and support. He agreed to help her. She explained exactly what the situation was and what she wanted to change. Woodsmall then told her exactly what to do to create the change.

"But I can't do that," she responded.

"Why?" he asked.

"Because it's not me," she explained.

Therein lies the problem. In order to create radical change in your life, you need to learn how to become "not me," and transform the person you are today. Maharishi Mahesh Yogi maintains that "the important thing is this: to be able, at any moment, to sacrifice what we are for what we could become."[1]

This doesn't mean you should deviate from your true self. In this case, it's the opposite.

By transforming and becoming "not me," you become your true, authentic self.

And through the process, you will realize that your limitations and self-defeating behavior are the results of programming that is built on a lie.

During this groundbreaking experience, you will:

- Understand why struggling isn't a key component to breaking through.

- Discover ways to optimize your energy.

- Determine your personal values and ensure that you are living in congruence with them.

- Learn why spirituality is a critical component to your success and happiness.

- Figure out how to identify your subconscious barriers and break free from them once and for all.

---

[1] See http://www.brainyquote.com/quotes/authors/m/maharishi_mahesh_yogi.html for more quotes from Maharishi Mahesh Yogi.

Denis Waitley says, "It's not what you are that holds you back, it's what you think you are not."[2] You may enter this experience thinking, "This is who I am," but you will leave with the tools to become a better version of yourself.

Are you ready to set fire to some of the misplaced beliefs of who you are and come out the other side feeling more fulfilled? Then, prepare to do what your soul is intended to do.

Let's begin.

---

[2] For more quotes from Denis Waitley, see http://www.goodreads.com/author/quotes/5108.Denis_Waitley.

Chapter 1

Are You Awake?

This is your last chance. After this, there is no turning back. You take the blue pill – the story ends, you wake up in your bed and believe whatever you want to believe. You take the red pill – you stay in Wonderland and I show you how deep the rabbit hole goes.

— Morpheus
from *The Matrix*[1]

[1] To read more quotes from The Matrix, see http://www.imdb.com/title/tt0133093/quotes.

Wake Up and Remember Who You Are

Do you have a memory that just sticks with you? I'm not talking about a big, show-stopping moment but, rather, a more subtle one—the kind that doesn't seem significant on the surface, but sparks a bigger "aha" moment when you examine it a little more closely.

My moment was in early elementary school in Buffalo Grove, Illinois, in what was my least favorite class since I had no voice for singing. Nonetheless, it remains to this day a vivid memory from my childhood. We were singing a song that encouraged us to accept and love ourselves the way we are. Strange as it may sound, this song was a bit of a wake-up call for me, but I was totally unaware of what to do with this information...yet.

It was in this moment I, as Gurdjieff calls it, "self-remembered."[2]

Your Soul is Tied to a Destiny

You see, most of us are in a state as if sleepwalking. We are literally unaware of ourselves and can't recognize that we are unique souls tied to a destiny... a purpose. Beyond that, we are not able to see ourselves as being capable to chart a course full of decisions. It is our ability to make decisions in the moment that truly orchestrates the outcomes in our lives. We have full capacity to manifest what we want, how we want to think, what we want to feel, and what specifically we want to do in the moment. At any time, in any place. Just set an intention in motion.

Our society today supports and reinforces a culture that is addicted to ongoing stimulus and activity. People have become absorbed in their lives, their stories, and their drama. Their minds are filled with ongoing circular chatter. They fail to realize they are in control. Rather, they live life like a character in someone else's movie.

This is not you, however. Obviously, you are different. The fact you are reading a book designed to improve yourself and make your life better, both personally and economically, sets you apart from the rest of the population. You can write, produce, and direct your own movie.

I want to share something with you that quite frankly is one of the top life-changing lessons I have learned.

In order to understand what I'm about to share, you will need to step back from yourself for a minute and see yourself from an unbiased perspective.

Here it is.

We are all living in a way that is aligned with our internal model of the world.

What Program Runs You?

A model of the world is our internal map of what we believe about ourselves, our lives, and how the world around us operates. It is not necessarily based on truth. In order for something to be true, it must exist 100 percent of the time. It doesn't shift due to circumstances or popular opinion.

Values are things that are aligned with our hearts. We can value our family, our health, our God, or our ability to contribute to a cause. We often navigate from what we think our values are and use them as rationale for our actions. Values are important.

That said, it is common for people to be incongruent with what they value and how they behave. Much of this is a parts problem, which we will address later. For now, I want you to consider the following quote from *A Course in Miracles:* "Appearances can but deceive the mind that wants to be deceived."[3]

We are running programs from our subconscious minds that cause us to continually manifest and create what we see as our "realities."

Artificial Paradigms

Everyone has paradigms[4] from which they live. The challenge with this? Many of these paradigms are not designed to empower the individual who is being held within them. Throughout history, society

---

[3] Helen Schucman and Bill Thetford, *A Course in Miracles*, "Chapter 30 The New Beginning," T-30.IV.6, http://www.unitedbeings.com/acim/Chapter%2030.htm.

has created and spread beliefs (some might call it propaganda) based on values and ideals that are designed specifically to control and manipulate people.

So how does this affect you? Let me share a client's story with you.

Rowing Together

Recently, a CEO named William[5] reached out to me because he was having some challenges with getting consistency in his organization. I sat down with him and his Executive Team to dig deeper into what paradigms might be taking place.

What I saw was a bunch of people playing their own politics. This happens quite a bit. Several members were operating within an artificial paradigm of what Patrick Lencioni calls "artificial harmony."[6] They weren't challenging the status quo and their performance was lackluster because no one wanted to rock the boat by bringing up concerns or complaints.

When people work together on an Executive Team, there is a natural tendency to protect their own interests and do what they feel is best for them, and not what is best for the team or the company. It doesn't really happen on a conscious level—it's more subconscious—and is most often driven from some type of dysfunctional behavior. Someone on the team needs to always be right—a clear indicator of self-esteem issues.

If everyone is acting like everything is okay, then I know that folks aren't being open and vulnerable with one another. When I sat with the team, I could tell that the members weren't actually on board, but they acted like they were because it was much easier than confronting the issues and having any conflict.

---

[4] Bob Proctor defines a paradigm as "a mental program that has almost exclusive control over our habitual behavior." For more information see http://bobproctorcoaching.com/.

[5] Names have been changed to protect the privacy of individuals.

[6] Patrick Lencioni, *The Five Dysfunctions of a Team* (San Francisco: Jossey-Bass, 2002).

To help break through, I coached William and his Executive Team on how they weren't being totally open and vulnerable with one another, and how they had created a lack of trust within the team. I also worked with each member independently in order to dive in and bring deeper personal issues to the surface.

After our work together, each member was able to show up in a more powerful way for the Executive Team meetings. They understood how their own insecurities had gotten in the way from being more open. They were also able to address the issues head-on (the elephant in the room) and it was clear that everyone was rowing together and working together at a much higher level.

It was incredible to see how all the members of the team were able to successfully remove their own self-interest and be more open, honest, and sincere with one another. By creating a healthy environment for conflict to be addressed within the team, we raised the standards of the company, which spread to managers and staff members. Today, the Executive Team is much more engaged and is performing at markedly higher levels.

The end result for William: a unified team at the top, which moved throughout other parts of his organization. By changing the paradigm of "artificial harmony," we were able to change the company's culture and increase the overall results.

Struggle is an Artificial Paradigm

Here is another example. In coaching CEOs, I have often seen the paradigm of thinking you must work hard and struggle to have success. In fact, without a struggle, some feel they are not truly worthy of the breakthrough.

Take a moment to think about what it means to struggle. In order to do so, some sort of resistance must be present. It is impossible to engage in a struggle without some type of physical push back. Why, then, do we often create our own resistance in the process of obtaining an outcome?

Causation and Effect

Dr. Wyatt Woodsmall shares that there are two common separate models of the world: the model of Causation and the model of Effect. The model of Causation says you create 100 percent of all the outcomes generated in your life. In fact, you have the ability to create and manifest whatever you truly desire. The model of Effect says that you are the end result in the world. In essence, things happen to you. People who live by this model blame other people and things to be responsible for what happens. This is the model of the world for victims. Most people in our world today live within the model of Effect. When things go wrong, they say things like "I was dealt a bad hand."

Accept Responsibility for Your Life

Before we go any further, I am going to hold your feet to the fire and ask you a question, What model of the world do you want to ascribe to? In order to even make the choice, you have to believe you actually have one.

Accepting responsibility for 100 percent of your life going forward is not the easiest road, but it is the only one to take if you wish to pursue personal mastery.

Some people are challenged by the idea of having to claim ownership and responsibility for everything that happens to them. What about the rape victim or the person who was severely beaten in an assault situation? It might seem uncompassionate to blame them for something so awful they could not have possibly chosen to happen to them.

I have instructed Sanchin-Ryu Karate for over twenty-five years, and in that time, I've been approached on several occasions by friends and people in the community who have experienced unfortunate circumstances. Many years ago, a friend of mine was beaten almost beyond recognition by two individuals on the street. He was walking home from a bar when the assailants approached him and unloaded their fists of fury. This guy ended up with a concussion, fractured ribs, and a broken nose. He reached out to me and asked for advice on what to do. Should he start studying a martial art too? Should he start concealing a weapon?

These conversations all lead to the same place. First and foremost, I say that it is necessary to accept responsibility for what happened. Often the person is bewildered by that response and retorts, *How can you say that?* I will then point out a choice that was made that led to the situation. In this case? Walking home at 1:00 a.m. on the streets of the city alone. A poor choice—even if someone is just "minding my own business."

Here is the issue: if you cannot accept responsibility for who and where you are, you will remain a victim. A victim is not empowered. I cannot help you if you choose to remain a victim.

You Always Have a Choice

As human beings, we all have a special gift. That gift is the power of choice. We can choose what to think, how to feel, and what to do. We make 35,000 decisions a day according to Quora.com. If most of these decisions are remotely conscious, imagine how many more are unconscious!

> *By becoming more awake and aware, we can begin to make better choices that are truly aligned with the world we wish to create.*

Imagine your ideal life. Where would you live? Who would you spend your time with? What things would you do? How would you live? What would your ideal day look like? Ideal week? Ideal month? Ideal year? Would your lifestyle be different? You can begin to make choices right here and now to make this a reality. Your journey toward this vision can start in a single moment with one action alone.

The action? Making a choice to pursue it.

In order to do so, you merely need to believe you deserve and can have whatever your heart desires. But you have to truly believe it. If you don't, you should question why. Where did that belief come from? Who told you? How did that person know? Remember, if what you believe does not occur 100 percent of the time in 100 percent of circumstances, it is not necessarily based on truth—it is an illusion.

As Tony Schwartz says, "Each of us shares an infinite capacity for self-deception."[7]

Change

What is required for you to choose to produce a new reality that is realigned with your ideal vision? CHANGE. That's it.

But change can be uncomfortable and cause friction in your world. Change is not popular. Change means becoming "not me." After all, it is who you are right now that is creating your current world and your current problems. Be warned. The people you have surrounded yourself with typically do not like it when you change.

One reason? Because the way they have controlled and manipulated you no longer works.

Illusion vs. Reality

I love the movie *The Matrix*. It draws on philosophical ideas from several texts, including Plato's *Allegory of the Cave*. In the movie, Neo is asked to choose to take a blue pill or a red pill. Take the blue pill and remain unaware and in the illusion of the Matrix, or take the red pill and escape the Matrix to the sometimes painful truth of reality. See how deep the rabbit hole goes?

Which pill will you choose? Do you believe you can make the choice of adopting the model of your world to be one of Causation? Or will your world remain in the model of Effect? Will you choose beliefs that truly empower you and are based on truth?

If so, follow me forward on the path of discovery, personal mastery, fulfillment, and leaving a legacy. It may not be a walk in the park. Rather, it might feel more like a fire walk. But I promise the breakthrough will be worth it.

Going Deeper

- Do you believe you have control of your fate?
- Is there anywhere you hold the illusion that someone or something is controlling you?

---

[7] Tony Schwartz, "Our Infinite Capacity for Self-Deception," Huffington Post, last updated November 17, 2011, http://www.huffingtonpost.com/tony-schwartz/our-infinite-capacity-for_b_174957.html.

Chapter 2

Are You Aligned?

*The consciousness of self is the greatest hindrance
to the proper execution of all physical action.*

— Bruce Lee[1]

---

[1] To read more quotes from Bruce Lee, see http://www.bruceleequotes.org/the-consciousness of-self-is-the-greatest-hindrance-to-the-proper-execution-of-all-physical-action/.

Why Are You Here?

One of the most profound questions you can ever ask yourself is, "Why am I here?"

Obviously, I don't mean why are you holding this book and reading it right now, but rather, I mean why are you here on this earth and in this lifetime?

Rick Warren offers a wake-up call to his readers in the first sentence of his best-selling book *The Purpose Driven Life: What on Earth am I Here For?* when he writes: "It's not about you."[2]

Shocker, right?

Using Warren's summation as a compass of sorts, you could view the "Why am I here?" question with the same lens. Your life's purpose is not about you. It is much bigger. In essence, it can be boiled down to two additional questions:

- What is your unique gift or talent?
- How can you use this gift to help others?

Your Mission and Vision

The intersection of what makes you unique and your ability to add value to others is where your life purpose—or mission—resides.

This mission is the driver that allows you to truly fulfill your vision. Your vision is the full scope of what you would like your life to look like.

Most people today don't have what they really want in their lives. The reason? They have no idea what they want. When I first heard this statement, I questioned the validity of it. Yet, if you ask people if they have a written vision of how they want their lives to look or a list of goals they would like to accomplish, you will find that very few do.

Grounding yourself with a compass that orients you is a major contributor to a life that is full of fulfillment and happiness.

[2] Rick Warren, *The Purpose Driven Life: What on Earth am I Here For?* (Grand Rapids: Zondervan, 2002), 5.

How important is vision? Imagine a rudderless ship setting sail. Wherever the wind goes…there you are. Now imagine a ship with a strong rudder, sail, and compass to point the direction. Which would you choose?

Goal Setting

I know that many people have heard of the idea of goal setting or vision casting but have never done it. So the question is, Why wouldn't they? Perhaps I should get more personal and ask, *Have YOU?* If you haven't, why not?

A 1979 Harvard study of graduate students found that the 3 percent of students who had clearly written down their goals went on to earn ten times as much money as the other 97 percent of students who either had no goals, or did have goals and/or a vision but had not written them down.[3]

Let's get back to "why not?" Some people simply struggle with their beliefs around setting goals. So, let me ask you this, point blank: Do you believe that your goals are possible? Do you believe you deserve these goals? How about believing in the process of writing them down? My intention is not to be critical, but rather to cast a light on your current beliefs and behavior.

What I have come to learn is that most people (yes, I am generalizing again) focus on what they *don't* want instead of what they *do* want, such as "I don't want debt" or "I don't want to be overweight" or "I don't want to be owned by my business."

There is a challenge with this level of thinking. Our subconscious mind does not understand or associate with the words "not"or "no." Instead, it hears the word "debt" and aligns with manifesting and generating more debt. Going forward, I challenge you to speak what you want, not what you don't want.

You want financial abundance of generating more money? Then claim it.

[3] Mark McCormack, What They DON'T Teach You at Harvard Business School: Notes from a Street-Smart Executive (New York: Bantam Books, 1984).

Cast Your Vision

You must believe that your vision is attainable. In order to do that, you have to overcome the challenges you are facing today by letting go of the thinking that holds those challenges in place. Change your perspective and look at the situation from a different position.

The past is NOT a predictor of your future, nor should it ever be.

If you don't 100 percent believe that your vision is possible, how do you know your disbelief is true? Where did that belief come from? It's merely a belief issue, so if it came from someone else, how do you know it is true for you?

Take the time to build a vision statement of the life you would like to live in the next three to five years. It is important to focus on your ideal life and the direction you want to go in, rather than what you want to leave or escape from. Energetically, it is much better to have a vision that pulls you forward. The more clarity the better.

Once you've outlined your vision, then take time on a regular basis to sit and visualize it. See yourself living the vision. Connect with what you see, hear, and feel. The more you can fully associate with the vision the better.

Vision Boards

An excellent strategy to connect with your vision is to build a book or vision board after you write out your vision. My wife, Jolie, and I started doing this about twelve years ago. It can be a very simple exercise.

Start by getting a piece of poster board. Set your intentions in motion and cut and paste pictures of how and where you would like to live and how you would like your life to look. The images can reflect a sense of being—peaceful, happy, fit—as well as material items, if you choose. The first year we did this, we hung our poster in the kitchen, where we were sure to see it. While we didn't necessarily sit and stare at it as we had our morning coffee, we certainly walked past it many times during the course of each day.

Eventually, we decided to sell the home we were living in and, for staging purposes, took our vision board down and packed it away. When we came across it a few years later, we were amazed to see just how many things on the vision board had come to reality. It really blew us away!

We were asked to be guest speakers at a business conference and during our talk about goal setting, Jolie and I showed the original vision board accompanied by a slide deck of actual photos of us having, doing, and embodying the ideas and images that were on our board. Powerful!

What is Your True North?

It's important to remember that your paradigm around visions should avoid deferment, such as "I will be happy when..." Being happy and having peace in your life will only come when you can adopt the model that *life is about the journey, not the destination.*

> ### *Yes, there certainly are destinations along the way, but enjoyment is aligned with loving the adventure.*

The key? Align your path with what you truly enjoy and where you can make an ongoing fulfilling contribution—your true north.

Don't Let Your Business Own You

Let's see how this plays out in real life. A CEO named Michael hired me about a year ago to coach him one-on-one because he wasn't happy even though his business was very successful. Michael worked 70 hours a week—days, nights, and weekends at times. He wasn't exercising as much as he wanted to. He wasn't spending time with his family like he wanted to. And he was feeling bitter and angry about it all.

He would be at work on a Thursday night and be upset because he wasn't with his family. Or, when he was spending time with his family he would feel guilty and anxious because he wasn't at work. He was agitated by everything he had to do—answer three hours of emails or tend to never-ending details of the business—and he always felt behind.

He simply wasn't living in harmony. He was burning out and he didn't know how to BREAK OUT. His business owned him.

Michael's challenge? He was looking at his world through the same perspective.

I helped him realize what paradigms were holding him back. He believed that in order for all these things to get done, they had to get done right, and in order for them to get done right, he had to do them. So, we identified all the tasks he was doing and he was able to see that he shouldn't have been doing some of them.

Then, we built additional systems around him that we could measure, and moved work off his plate to other staff members. The tasks that remained for him to complete highlighted his brilliance and brought him joy. As Michael began doing more of what he liked and took pleasure in, he wasn't as resentful.

This new perspective helped Michael to shift and find his true north. It helped him understand that he had to be in the moment where he was. He learned that wherever he was, he needed to focus on that and be there.

The takeaway: Just be where you are.

After one year, our work together created a new world for him with peace, freedom, and happiness. He began working 45 to 50 hours a week in areas where he was highly productive and he had more love for what he was doing. AND his business continued to grow in double digits. Because Michael was now working on things that he enjoyed doing, his animosity and anger went away and his business didn't own him anymore.

Many of the executives I've coached are not enjoying the journey, just like Michael. Oftentimes, this comes from one of two places: they no longer like what they are doing (stemming from either what they do or who they are working with) or their lives are out of balance.

Life Balance

In order to create an empowering paradigm, we need to establish our own personal definition of life balance and what it truly means for us. The answer is different for everyone. However, the elements are typically the same. Water always finds its own level; the universe is perfectly balanced to sustain life.

What is it that we are trying to balance anyway?

Think of a "life wheel" with spokes that can be drawn from our life departments: Faith, Health and Wellness, Family, Business, Finances, Friends, and Environment. It is more than just how much physical time we dedicate to each of these areas, but also how much of our mental, emotional, and physical resources are being dedicated. Rate where you think you are on a scale of one to ten in each department. Any department that has a lower number can be labeled "out of balance," much like a wheel that has one or more bent or broken spokes.

Likewise, we can think of balance from a martial arts perspective. Bruce Lee asserts, "Martial arts, like any art, is an unrestricted athletic expression of an individual soul."[4] I agree.

What to Focus On

I distinctly remember a shift in my thinking that came from a conversation with the Chief Grand Master of Sanchin-Ryu Karate. I asked him how to prevent loss of balance in a physical confrontation. He said that I should spend more time training in how to regain balance than in how to *not* lose balance. If we are working to *not* lose balance, we are in a state of defense and are often reactive. In this state, loss of balance is inevitable. If we close the window from focusing on loss of balance to being re-centered, we will be able to have much more fluidity in our movement.

We can apply this context to the physical, mental, emotional, and spiritual areas of our lives. I help my clients define what it means to have personal balance in all of these areas.

We must first know what it means to be re-centered in order to regain balance in our lives.

---

[4] To read more quotes from Bruce Lee, see http://www.azquotes.com/quote/628312.

In order to do this you have to assign meaning to experience. In *Man's Search for Meaning*, Viktor Frankl, a holocaust survivor, found a way to re-center his mindset to find meaning in even the most brutal existence.[5] You, too, have the ability to assign meaning to anything in your life. If you don't, then you will become off balance.

Once you understand that centered means balanced means equanimity, then you can appreciate that happiness requires the same attention and understanding as sadness. Knowing this opens the door for gratitude and grace.

Gratitude

Gratitude comes from the Latin root word *gratia*, meaning grace, graciousness, and gratefulness. It is directly tied to the universal law of Cause and Effect, which we will talk more about in Chapter 3, and is super foundational for what you can do in your life. Several studies on gratitude have demonstrated how it can lead to increased well-being, better sleep, and even lower physical pain in those who practice it often.[6]

So what is gratitude? It's a feeling of being thankful, for even the smallest thing in your life. It's the experience of counting your blessings.

In the concentration camp, Frankl found that the prisoners who focused on the good in something—whatever it was—had more longevity. This goes back to mindset, and assigning meaning to acontext. Frankl kept his own mind focused on things that brought him joy, and his gratitude came from the fact that the guards couldn't take away his ability to think or what he thought about.

If you're stuck, then you are focusing on what's wrong and you are not practicing gratitude. We always have freedom of choice even in the midst of severe suffering. At times, pain in our lives may not

---

[5] Viktor Frankl, Man's Search for Meaning (New York: Washington Square Press, 1959).

[6] R.A. Emmons, et al. "Counting Blessings Versus Burdens: An Experimental Investigation of Gratitude and Subjective Well-Being in Daily Life," Journal of Personality and Social Psychology (Feb. 2003): Vol. 84, No. 2, pp. 377–89 and A.M. Grant, et al. "A Little Thanks Goes a Long Way: Explaining Why Gratitude Expressions Motivate Prosocial Behavior," Journal of Personality and Social Psychology (June 2010): Vol. 98, No. 6, pp. 946–55.

be a choice, but suffering is. No matter what you experience, grace and gratitude is present.

Align Your Parts

The largest obstacle that exists when it comes to changing our behavior and achieving life balance can be found in the separate parts of ourselves.[7] Each of us has a part that wants change and another part that is being served by the current circumstance. For instance, I have worked with clients who want to make new choices in diet and exercise. Part of them wants to be in better shape and have better health, yet part of them is served by poor food choices and an idle life style. Their food selections bring them a sense of comfort or control in an otherwise chaotic home or work life.

Similarly, I have other executive clients who want to spend more time and energy to grow their company, but they also want to spend more time with their families and have Fridays off in the summer.

Until these parts are united and realigned, you will continue to live in conflict.

Going Deeper

- What is the vision for your life professionally and personally?
- What parts of yourself need to be aligned?

---

[7]As a NLP Practitioner, I often use the theoretical element of the separate parts of ourselves that was introduced to me by one of my mentors, Dr. Wyatt Woodsmall.

Chapter 3

Are you Clear?

What is real? How do you define 'real'? If you're talking about what you can feel, what you can smell, what you can taste and see, then 'real' is simply electrical signals interpreted by your brain.

—Morpheus
from *The Matrix*[1]

---

[1] For more quotes from The Matrix, see http://www.imdb.com/title/tt0133093/quotes.

You Are Not Alone

No, this is not an advertisement for the next *Close Encounters* movie, though it was a childhood favorite! Rather, this is an invitation to adopt one of the most empowering personal paradigms: spirituality.

Let's review. You have the ability to choose the beliefs that frame your specific model of the world. Once you begin to operate at a higher level of consciousness, you have the ability to choose beliefs that are most empowering to you.

The belief that there is a God and the context behind this belief have a major impact on you.

Please note: When I speak of God, I am not directing you to a specific religion. God is whatever holds the most meaning for you. You might call God *the Universe, Higher Power, the Light, Nature,* or some other name that has significance for you. What is important is that you understand God to be something that is a source. And remember, everything or everyone's version of God isn't yours.

Faith Equals Power

Now, why is this belief so compelling? By believing in God, you are truly more resourceful and capable.

> *Believing in God allows you the ability to leverage an additional power beyond yourself that can assist you in your life's purpose and vision.*

Faith is extremely moving. Without it, no great thing is ever accomplished. Faith is having certainty when there is no current physical evidence that what you seek exists. It's like the pull of gravity or breathing air—we know it's there, even if we cannot see it.

Each of us uses faith on a regular basis. Each time we get in the car and drive, we exercise faith that other people will stay in their lanes, a safe distance away, and not run into us. We exercise faith that the food is fresh and not tainted when we order a meal at a restaurant.

The challenge we run into is that we don't employ faith when it relies on us. This issue goes deeper into our concept of self, our self-love, and our own internal sense of creating security.

What Do You Believe In?

How we think about God also orients how we live. So, I ask you, *What are your beliefs about God?*

Many of you may find these beliefs in the writings or doctrines of others. Regardless, I suggest that you question everything that you are told with a mind that seeks the truth.

A belief in something greater that is built on another's perspective and not your own experience is a shallow well.

Once we have a solid model of the world that is centered on our relationship with God, it is time to develop a true relationship. God can work through you if you allow it to happen. The challenge is that many of us are too busy living our lives and being engaged in our businesses to tap in and listen. We have been conditioned to not tune in and are addicted to activity and technology that radically draws our attention outward.

God is the creator of all things and connected to all.

Your connection with God comes from within—the same place your personal truth resides.

Stop the Noise

We all have a silent, strong, inner knowing that is guided from our intuition. It is something that is easily accessible, but you must first tune in and stop all the external and internal noise you are creating.

So how do you do this? The best way is to surrender to God and listen. You have to align your soul with God to get to where you want to go. If you listen, you will be able to hear the messages and get clear on what you are supposed to do. How many times has God been trying to call you, but the line is busy and God can't get through? Listening means surrendering. You have to put your faith in a higher power to become connected. Try it. Just sit and listen.

Being able to navigate your life with a deep connection to God in a way that is connected to your purpose is a transformative experience. It allows you to have fulfillment while you enjoy the journey. Additionally, it gives your life meaning.

Frames of Reference

In NLP, we talk about the term *frame of reference* as shaping your decision-making process and the way you evaluate yourself and your personal performance.

There are two basic frames of reference—internal and external—and each has its own complications if taken to the extreme. For example, deeply rooted motivators like culture, family values, and religion are strong influences in your programmed internal frame of reference. If your frame of reference is to the extreme either way, it can be difficult to reprogram, but it can and should be done.

People with an **internal frame of reference** use themselves as motivation for their actions and decisions. They don't wait for approval from outside influences or base their own success or self-worth on other people's opinions. They are confident and powerful risk takers. The challenge with the extreme side of an internal frame of reference is the potential to become conceited and over-confident, not noticing other people or outside situations that may offer valuable insight or information.

Those with an **external frame of reference** require much direction and encouragement. They often ask what others think and base their decisions or value on outside sources. Those with an extreme external frame of reference are not capable of motivating themselves or making their own choices because they are more concerned with what someone else thinks and take criticism very personally.

Balancing the Two Frames of Reference

The most constructive balance of the two frames of reference is to mostly rely on your internal frame with recognition that there are times when you need to allow room for external influence in certain situations. For example, having an open mind to new information or learning a new skill requires an external frame of reference. The solution lies in your ability to determine which frame of reference is required of you in any given situation.

Listen to Your Soul

So how does this relate to God and connecting to your purpose?

> ### *The key to spirituality is having an internal frame of reference that is connected to your soul.*

If our concern lies primarily with what other people will think about the decision we are making, we are no longer listening to our soul.

An ancient Vedic Sanskrit saying offers another way for us to understand this: *Humans are physical, spiritual beings in a meaningful and purposeful universe of unlimited consciousness.*

Universal Laws

It is all about getting clear. At times things seem blurry. What is it that causes the fog to lift? It is your ability to connect with a truth. A truth is something that has to be true 100 percent of the time, in all situations and at all times. These truths are also known as universal laws.

You probably have heard of the Law of Attraction, but did you know that some traditions talk of twelve or even twenty-one universal laws?[2] It is beneficial to be aware of these truths because additional beliefs and paradigms that you will find empowering are aligned with them.

Universal laws are worth studying and are not tied to any specific religion. In fact, you will find them represented in all major religions.

The Law of Cause and Effect

One of the key universal laws is the Law of Cause and Effect. This law allows you to step into the model of the world that I mentioned in Chapter 1, which is built on Causation. You are the cause and everything happens based on what you do. Gratitude is tied closely to cause and effect.

[2] Henk J.M. Schram, "The Universal Law of Attraction—How Many Universal Laws Are There Anyway?" e-zine articles, May 31, 2007, http://ezinearticles.com/?The-Universal-Law-of-Attraction---How-Many-Universal-Laws-Are-There-Anyway?&id=585401.

Your ability to produce outcomes that are aligned with your vision will be in direct correlation to leveraging the Law of Cause and Effect

The Law of Polarity

Another important universal law is the Law of Polarity, which states that there are two sides to everything. For instance, there is a hot and a cold, light and dark. There is a front and a back to this page in the book that you are reading. If you were to split or cut it any number of ways, there would still be a front and back.

Napoleon Hill, author of the classic *Think and Grow Rich* published in 1937, writes, "Every adversity, every failure and every heartache carries with it the seed of an equivalent or a greater benefit."[3] This is the essence of the Law of Polarity.

While there are other universal laws, we won't go into them now. Just be aware that they exist, and that they hold a lot of power to help you set your intentions in motion.

Work vs. Family

Life presents challenges to us sometimes. Let's say, for example, your relationship with your spouse is currently strained because you haven't been actively nurturing the relationship or investing the time that is necessary for your spouse to feel connected and loved. I have seen this challenge manifested many times with my clients. The driver of the problem is that they are spending more time growing the business than they are spending with their families.

Is there an opportunity in this situation? Yes. Transformation. While you cannot be in more than one place at a time, the paradigm behind not being able to do both effectively needs to be challenged.

> *There is enough time to do everything if we make it a priority in our lives.*

Many of my clients come to me working 60 to 70 hours a week and pull in a sizeable income. I also have clients that make over twice that and do so working 40 or fewer hours a week.

[3] Napoleon Hill, Think and Grow Rich (Minneapolis: Filiquarian Publishing, 2005).

To become the person who can transform, you have to be someone who can be a CEO and is also dedicated to your family. It's that simple.

Whenever you have a need, the solution to that need must also exist at the same time.

I suggest you some spend time studying universal laws and become acquainted with them. As you move forward, look at situations and ask yourself what the reality is behind them. The key is confirming whether or not your thoughts are based on truth. For something to be true (yes, I am repeating this), it MUST exist 100 percent of the time...not just sometimes.

Attention

So, how do we create a deeper connection with God? This is a profound and perplexing question. Nothing can replace your experience. This is your personal journey. *The key to unlocking the door is how and where you direct your attention.*

But if you believe in God, then you have something greater to leverage—a higher power to rely on so you don't have to do it on your own to get to where you want to go. In order to commune with our creator, we must be able to focus our attention in a specific way. It's hard to have a conversation with God when your mind is focused on everything else.

Your time and energy must be directed. Prayer and meditation are two powerful ways to do this. They can help to create stillness in your mind. Yoga, Tai Chi, and meditation have helped me personally in this capacity. By keeping the focus on a key point or stilling the mind all together, you can tune yourself like an instrument. Knowing that "The kingdom of God is within you"[4] can be a powerful internal frame of reference. In order to remember that, you can say to yourself, "Be still and know that I am God."[5]

Another way to focus your attention is to admit you're powerless over what it is you need or want to conquer. Ask God for help and pray and meditate on it every day. Talk to other like-minded people about it.

4 Luke 17:20-21.
5 Psalms 46:10.

Take your hands "off the wheel," so to speak, and then do the work that supports the ideal version of you.

Usually, when I talk about quieting the mind and carving out time to meditate, I am often met with resistance. It seems counterproductive to carve out time to seemingly do nothing when one of your greatest challenges can be getting things done. This is an illusion.

Jack Canfield, in his Success Principles seminars, teaches that one hour of personal internal work is worth seven hours of external work.

> *This moment is a gift.*
> *What you do with it is your decision.*
> *You can fill your calendar to the max*
> *and work hard. Work your ass off.*
> *And totally miss the mark.*

Let's get real here. Let me ask you again, *What is your life purpose?* What is your life about? When you pass on—which is inevitable, by the way—how would you like to be remembered?

We avoid the topic in our society but it is the truth. You and I will die someday. All of us will. Today is all we have.

Where your attention goes, energy flows. Start today.

Going Deeper

- What do you believe your life is about?
- What universal laws are you incongruent with?

Chapter 4

Are You Resourceful?

By research analysis, actually only 35 percent of the public is really interested in truth for its own sake.

—David Hawkins[1]

---

[1] David R. Hawkins, Truth vs. Falsehood: How to Tell the Difference (Toronto: Axial Publishing Company, 2005).

Where Are You vs. Where Do You Want To Be?

As we discussed in the last chapter, it is not common for people to orientate themselves in a way that aligns with their truths. Rather they are heavily influenced, conditioned, and programmed by what other people think.

We create stories to justify our model of the world.

They key? Stay awake. The more you are self-aware, the easier it is to make the changes necessary to move in the direction you want to go. Be resourceful.

What does it mean to be resourceful? Loosely, it can be defined as "of source," which means keeping connected to God and working off your intuition. In order to make progress in a way that has grace and flow, it is helpful to work with the grain instead of against it.

Once we have clarity in where we want to go and the faith to pursue it, we need to make an honest assessment of where we are against where we want to be. Imagine you are dropped off in the desert with a map, supplies for survival, and a specific destination in mind. The helicopter lands, your blindfold is removed, and it is just you, your supplies, and your map. Only you do not have a GPS and when you spin around you are surrounded by hills of sand. The sky is overcast and there is no sun. It is very difficult to guide yourself to your destination if you do not know where you are.

Where are you in this moment? Is your current reality where you want to be?

Alignment

A few years ago, a CEO named Dana contacted me because her Executive Team wasn't performing at a level that she preferred and her company wasn't where she wanted it to be. When I asked her what she thought might be going on, she didn't know, but told me how each member of her team had the utmost loyalty and had been with her through thick and thin.

One of the ways I like to find out what is happening is to interview different members of the team and look for consistency—to see if they

29

are all in the same game and if they are all focused on the same thing. So, I went around and asked each member questions such as *What's really important?* and *What is it that you are focusing on right now?* and *What's important for this year?*

I found that there was an inconsistency in how the company was being run, which affected the environment and culture within it. The thing about teams is that you are limited to the potential of the people on that team. Each person needs to be growing individually—if not, it holds the company back. And each member needs to be focused on the same goal.

Think of it in another way—like the New England Patriots. I know not everyone out there is a football fan, but New England folks love their Patriots! So, when the offense is on the field and Brady has the ball, there is one objective—to score. But regardless of that, the strategy is to move the ball down the field. Each player on the team knows exactly how far they have to go based on that point in time. There really isn't any question. Everyone is on the same page, on the same field, and working toward the same goal. So, they basically call the strategy for the best play.

Have you ever heard of the classic book *Good to Great*, in which Jim Collins says, "To build a successful organization and team, you must get the right people on the bus"?[2]

Within Executive Teams, the mindset behind the objective has to be the strategy of how each member is going to accomplish it. Is everyone on the same page with the strategy? What is the system that the team is using to do that?

So, ask yourself, do you really have the right people in the right seats (the right places) on the bus? Do you need to get people off the bus or move people to different seats in order to help them develop the best parts of themselves?

It's a constant process of calibration. When I met with the members of Dana's Executive Team, I got a feel right away if they were the right

[2] Jim Collins, Good to Great: Why Some Companies Make the Leap...and Other's Don't (New York: HarperBusiness, 2011).

people in the right seats. Even though it was difficult, I let Dana know that one person needed to exit the bus. Dana had been so blinded by her own paradigms—loyalty and her own past—that she couldn't see the effect this person was having on the team and on her company. Through this alignment process, I helped Dana realize how this person was limiting them.

You have to look at the future from the future. You can't get there from where you are. As long as you are stuck looking at the future from where you are and the past that you came from, your perspective is going to be limited.

The breakthroughs that happened on Dana's Executive Team after our work together were tremendous! A freedom and lightness transcended throughout the company. The alignment helped the bottom line, helped the top line, and resulted in a new culture where everyone experienced more fun and productivity at work.

Your Current Reality

You see, your current reality is not a mistake. It was very intentional. Though you are not conscious of the intention, *what* you are doing and *who* you are being is causing the results you want to change. So, what results are you creating that are not aligned with your ideal vision? What thoughts and beliefs are behind the behavior that is currently keeping you where you are?

People, places, and things either suck energy from us or give us energy. It is our objective to be conscious of what they are and why.

Restricting Beliefs

One of the things that can suck your energy is a restricting belief—something that you decide is true but somehow limits your potential. The two biggest restricting beliefs are: what you think is possible and what you believe you are capable of. Know that it is okay to create "what it could be" if you had unlimited resources and a magic wand even if it sounds impossible to you.

If you suspend your restricting beliefs, then amazing things can happen. So, take your paradigm and put it on hold. Act entirely in correlation with a different paradigm and watch what can happen.

When you let go of thinking
something is impossible,
you find out what is truly possible.

Most of our limitations are in our mind.

We often see the world the way we want it to be. We distort the world because we want it to somehow meet our beliefs and values, even if they are restricting. Reality is not the problem—it is our perception of reality that is the problem.

What is Keeping You Stuck?

I learned a great exercise from one of my coaches, Tom Shields, that illustrates this. Let's say you want to spend time working out. Yet, you never seem to get to it. Instead of focusing on what you need to do, you say, "Walk me through the process of what happens when I don't work out."

How do you do that exactly? Now imagine that I am going to be you tomorrow and I have committed to work out. Only I am not going to follow through. Why? What thoughts do I think? What pictures and movies are in my head? What things do I say to myself? What do I say and do that keeps me from following through?

I know this idea seems counterintuitive, yet everything we do has a strategy. There is a way to procrastinate. It involves thoughts we think, feelings we generate, and actions we end up taking.

If you can "unpack" the process of what you think, hear, say and do, it is easier to break the pattern that is keeping you stuck and install a new strategy.

A Problem is Not Really a Problem

You cannot solve a problem with the same level of consciousness you had when the problem was created. In other words, as long as you see things the same way, you will continue to consistently approach a problem with the same level of thinking that holds it in place.

But you see, problems don't really exist. They are an illusion.

In reality a problem is not a problem to begin with. In order to create a problem we need to assign a specific meaning or context to a particular situation. This is why two people might have the same exact circumstance, but one sees it as a problem and the other sees it as an opportunity. You have to give a problem a framework in order for it to exist.

Envision Your Ideal Future

A bridge must be built from where you are today to where you want to be tomorrow. Think of a bridge you have driven or walked over. Before it was built, someone once set a goal to create an improved route. In order to do so they needed a reason why.

It all begins with the vision, or the picture we hold in the mind's eye of how we want the future to look. Let's walk into the theater of your mind. Grab a seat.

Close your eyes after reading this paragraph and see yourself watching your ideal future. Create a scene and make the movie brilliant color, 3D, and surround sound. Watch this scene of your life. Then step into the movie. Be in it. See what you see, hear what you hear, feel what you feel. Are there any smells or tastes associated with it? The more vivid you can make it the better.

Seeing your future in advance is a powerful exercise to help you build a sturdy bridge to the future you most want.

Timelines

Our mind can go several places—the past, the future, daydreaming, and in the now. All of these areas serve a purpose to us. Yet, we are often not aware where we are directing our attention.

Timeline work is a great strategy that I learned from NLP. If I asked you to point to the future, which direction would you point? Ahead? Above? To the right? How about the past? Behind you? To the left? Below? Where is now? Are you in it? Is it just in front of you?

We create these kinds of associations in the context of how we think about time. The mind constantly moves from past, to future, to the present moment. People who are strategic planners and are constantly thinking ahead are operating in what is called *through time*. People who are in the moment are characterized as being *in time* and are often late to things because they are fully engrossed in what they are doing and are not watching the time.

Yet, both of these timelines are solid strategies we should employ. The truth is that time does not exist. Time is a human concept. We use it to measure and plan. It was a brilliant invention, but we get caught in paradigms and strategies that are not empowering when we think about time.

Past or Future

One of the key ideas that I use with my clients is that the emotions we generate come from a timeline. For example, regret comes from thinking about the past. Anxiety comes from worrying about the future. When we think this way, we get into non-empowering "loops" that ultimately create our moods.

But it doesn't have to be that way. Think of a tree's timeline—the tree's rings show the history of the tree. Did it live through drought or plentiful rain and sun? Instead of getting caught in its past loops of history, the tree simply records its resourcefulness.

The interesting thing is that:

Once we become aware that WE are generating our own emotions from our own timelines, we can stop doing the things that don't empower us and do something else.

The future is the place to plan and strategize. The past is the place that holds memories and lessons learned. Many people use the past as a storehouse of pain. They continue to recreate events or situations that have been assigned a negative context (playing the role of a victim), and then play the movie over and over in their heads.

Pay attention to how you are using your timeline. Where are you spending your mental and emotional energy? Is it helping you to achieve your ideal outcome?

The Present

There is a whole movement today in mindfulness. In order to practice mindfulness you must be in the present moment and focused on what is at hand. If you want to be happy, happiness is created in the present moment.

I always ask my clients if they want to enroll in the school of Enjoy the Journey. If this is something you want, then I challenge you to have peace and fulfillment on the way. The goal is to optimize your performance, but to do so with ease, flow, grace, and joy.

Where will the resources for your bridge to the future come from? The only place change can occur is in the now.

Going Deeper

- What beliefs/paradigms do you have that are holding you back?
- What needs to happen or what must you know and understand for you to shift the paradigm/belief?

Chapter 5

Who Do You Need To Become?

Enslavement by illusion is comfortable;
it is the liberation by Truth that people fear.

—David Hawkins[1]

[1] David R. Hawkins, Truth vs. Falsehood: How to Tell the Difference (Toronto: Axial Publishing Company, 2005).

What is "Work" to You?

My brother-in-law and I have become interested in fat tire bikes that you can ride not only in the snow, but also on the beach. I love investing resources in ways to enjoy the outdoors and stay in shape. On one of our vacations, my brother-in-law and I rode the bikes along the Lake Michigan shoreline and encountered three different people who commented on the amount of effort we needed to ride our bikes on the beach and said, "That looks like too much work."

I responded, "Of course it takes effort and that is why it's an amazing way to get exercise!"

This experience exemplifies one of our country's many paradigms surrounding "work." Work has become a negative connotation. "Don't work too hard."

What do you believe about work? Do you often use the adjective "hard" in the same sentence? There is a common belief in our society that in order "get ahead," (What the hell is that anyway? Are you behind?) you must put forth a high effort. Maybe it's a matter of deservedness. Perhaps you feel that you can't have nice things or success unless you have "earned it." Each level of worthiness can be different.

Work and effort is not necessarily a bad thing. Think of an artist whose work is to paint. Painting is joyful to them, so the work is effortless. Or think of a relationship with your soul mate. Relationships take work, yet because of the immense love and bond between you, it is done mostly with ease. Think of it another way: Water requires no effort to carve stone. It simply seeks balance. Nothing can stop the flow of water, unless it changes form. If rock happens to get in the way and stay there long enough, water will effortlessly change the rock.

So, what is the problem with work? Well…there shouldn't be a problem.

Flow vs. Struggle

I teach my Karate students how to flow in the heat of battle instead of being rigid. Imagine tightening all your muscles and then committing to a physical movement, such as a punch, while you maintain the rigidity. How fast would you be able to move? How well would you be able to flow from technique to technique? You wouldn't be able to. Rather you would be choppy and slow and struggle to do each physical movement.

If you have to push through and force your way to the outcome, then resistance must be evident. Where is this resistance coming from?

Consider this: What would achieving results feel like if you could do so with less effort? Imagine more ease and grace with your outcomes.

Deepak Chopra refers to the Law of Least Effort, or the fact that nature's intelligence functions with effortless ease.[2] How much does a plant struggle to grow? The strategy of this law is to minimize the effort and maximize our results.

Why We Struggle

So why do we continue to struggle to get what we want? Here's a great example of a recent client. An Executive in his fifties named Robert had a successful company and created a lot of income for himself, but he was working his guts out. He was in shape, exercised, and ate well, but he worked and worked…and worked. And he worked much harder than he needed to.

There was active resistance going on within him. When I asked him to work on a question or a homework assignment, he would spend a huge amount of time on it and always go the extra mile—sometimes sending me a diary. He had to make everything harder and more complicated than it needed to be. But he "needed to get it right."

I could see that he had some programming—we all have programming—that "in order to get ahead, or have success, you have to struggle." He truly believed this. And this paradigm was holding him back. He would take a situation that was easy and going well, and he would make it complicated. He had to struggle to get ahead. He had to have constant resistance and problems in his life and his company, which he continually manifested.

[2]Also see http://www.chopra.com/the-law-of-least-effort.

38

In addition, Robert was living with another paradigm. He believed "You don't deserve the money you make unless you work hard," which overlapped with the struggle.

We worked together to shift his paradigms by highlighting how they weren't based in truth or fact, and that they were actually based in BS. Once he realized this, Robert's life became so much more enjoyable. He became lighter and was able to produce the best year in his company (it grew something like 30 to 40 percent!), while he worked less than he did before.

Think about that—working less, making more money, not working as hard or struggling, and enjoying it. Robert did this because he adjusted the lens from which he was operating.

It's important that someone points out the beliefs/paradigms that you are holding in your life and the wiring/programming from which you operate because as long as you have them, you're going to continue to operate from that place. It doesn't matter what you change.

> ### *Unless you shift these paradigms/beliefs at a deeper level, you will always go back from whence you came.*

Resistance

So, what causes flow versus struggle?

Resistance happens when we meet internal opposition. Struggle occurs when we typically work against universal laws, try to control things that are out of our influence of control, or we simply assign unrealistic rules to how things are or aren't.

An example is the resistance of getting older and not having things change. One of the key doctrines in Buddhism is that of impermanence. Impermanence tells us that things are in constant change or flux. In life nothing stays the same. Yet as humans we typically do not like change. If we choose to fight the change, then we create our own struggle or suffering.

In order for something to work with ease, there has to be lack of resistance.

Yes, we can experience pain with chronic conditions, yet the suffering associated with the pain is a choice.

Self-Actualization

In 1943 Abraham Maslow defined his Hierarchy of Needs.[3] These needs are described in a five-stage model that outlines a human's ability to grow. The base level is rooted in needs for basic survival. When you meet one level, you are able to move onto the next.

The peak level (number 5) is "Self-Actualization," when you can remove insecurities and are able to function in an optimal space. I often equate this level with someone who is capable of operating on purpose in life with little or no stress.

It was massively liberating once I realized that I was creating my own problems and causing my own frustration.

The key is to be awake. When we are asleep and unconscious we fall into our own traps.

So, what is an initial step?

In order to overcome struggle and resistance and become self-actualized, surrendering is the very first step. Once you are aware, you must be willing to surrender, admit that you need to change, and rely on your higher power or God. Being in the flow from whatever and wherever it comes, you can experience something real and powerful.

Your True Self

A core way to live a happy, fulfilled, and enriching life is to live according to your true self. What is your true self? It is the *essence* of who you really are at the heart and soul level. Not who you *believe* you are, which is connected to your head.

---

[3] To read more about Maslow's Hierarchy of Needs, see Saul McLeod, "Maslow's Hierarchy of Needs," Simply Psychology (2007), last updated 2014, http://www.simplypsychology.org/maslow.html.

When Michelangelo was asked how he made the statue David—one of the most famous sculptures in existence—he explained that he merely started with a giant piece of marble and took away everything that was not David.[4] Your evolution is similar.

> *By working on yourself, reprogramming your beliefs, and acting in new ways that are more empowering and liberating, you allow yourself to let go of the struggle and become who you really are.*

This is the path to Self-Actualization.

Going Deeper

- What is creating struggle in your life?
- Where is your resistance coming from?

---

[4] Lori Deschene, "Tiny Wisdom: Taking Things Away," http://tinybuddha.com/quotes/tiny-wisdom-what-we-choose-to-take-away/.

Chapter 6

Are You Empowered?

Instead, you ought to say, "If it is the Lord's will, we will live and do this or that."[1]

[1] James 4:15.

Optimum Performance

Your ability to perform at high levels and optimize yourself to be efficient is in direct correlation to mastering yourself and reaching your true potential.

Tony Schwartz said that we're not meant to run at high speeds, continuously, for long periods of time.[2] Science tells us we're at our best when we move rhythmically between spending and renewing energy. I could not agree more. There is a key balance needed to ensure we are running optimally.

So, what does it take?

Discipline

On a professional level, I have been working out of a home office ever since I began my first job twenty-three years ago. I invariably come across people who tell me how they "could never do that." When I ask them why not, the answer is something like, "I wouldn't get anything done." Or, "I can't discipline myself to do that." My first thought is YIKES.

According to Raymond Holliwell,

"Discipline is the high road that makes life worth living."[3]

Our talent comes from developing discipline. Just like an athlete, an artist, or an Executive Business leader, the more you have specific intentions for yourself, the better you get. The better you get, the easier your life becomes.

Making clear and specific choices is a conscious process. Just like I made the decision to sit down and write on a Sunday afternoon while the Patriots were playing—it's a choice. I can choose to watch the game or I can choose to follow through on the commitment I made to write this book so that I can offer value to those of you who seek it.

[2] See http://theenergyproject.com/key-ideas.

[3] Raymond Holliwell, Working with the Law: Powerful Principles for Abundant Living, http://dreamingtribe.com/wp-content/uploads/2014/04/working-with-the-law-raymondholliwell-pdf.pdf

Some people think that discipline means that you have to make a great "sacrifice." You might even know people who are seeking optimum health but make an unhealthy choice at a party. Why? Maybe because they think it offers an experience of a kind of "freedom." But are they truly free? Aren't they sacrificing the right kind of energy or their long-term health for short-term pleasure? We all will sacrifice something. There is no doubt about it.

The question is, *What is more important?*

You see, discipline is never an option. We just have the illusion that it is. Discipline is our ability to self-direct ourselves mentally, emotionally, and physically. We either discipline ourselves or someone else eventually will.

Self-Control

My wife Jolie and I recently looked at preschools for our daughter. One Director explained how their school's educational model emphasizes individual self-control. She also stated that the less control a child is able to demonstrate in life, the more the child will need some form of outside control. The more we can discipline ourselves internally, the less we need to be disciplined externally.

The first step to developing discipline is having awareness and becoming conscious of what you are thinking, feeling, and doing. Once we are able to self-observe, we can truly accept responsibility for all of our actions and then correct our course.

Live in integrity with the actions and commitments that are congruent with the outcomes you wish. If you struggle with this, get a good coach or consultant to help you. Make sure this is someone who lives what he or she teaches.

Bob Proctor says it perfectly, "Discipline is giving yourself a command and following it up with action."[4]

Consistency

People are often fascinated when I tell them that I have been studying

---

[4] For more quotes from Bob Proctor, see https://www.goodreads.com/author/quotes/72625.Bob_Proctor.

Martial Arts consistently for nearly thirty years. Yes, it takes discipline. But, truth be told, it hasn't been all that difficult for me. Neither has working out on a regular basis nor making conscious decisions around what foods I put into my body.

> *My wife and I realized that in order*
> *for us to have longevity and*
> *live fulfilling lives that are full of joy,*
> *we had better get educated and clear*
> *on what it takes to live in a healthy way.*

Health and Wellness

When it comes to health and wellness there are several schools of thought. However, if you are willing to seek the truth, do the research, and think for yourself, you can take ownership of your health and well-being.

Many people I know personally put their doctors on a pedestal and take their word for gospel because they have a medical degree. If a doctor has all the answers, then why is it so easy to find another doctor with different opinions and prognoses for the same condition?

I am not against the medical community, but I think some of us place way too much power in the hands of someone else instead of managing our own well-being. Take an active role and get educated when it comes to your own health and wellness.

It's an absolute priority!

Taking medications that are designed to curb symptoms and not get to the root of the cause is a slippery slope. You need to find what natural ways work best to get you in a place where you have little or no health ailments so that you can enjoy your life.

Here are the top six areas I suggest you dial in:

1) Sleep

Enough research has shown that you need a minimum of seven to eight hours of sleep every night.[5] Yes, you may feel you can get by

---

[5] "How Much Sleep Do We Really Need?" National Sleep Foundation, https://sleepfoundation.org/how-sleep-works/how-much-sleep-do-we-really-need.

with less, but what your body does while you are sleeping cannot be replaced in any other way.

Sleep deprivation[6] negatively impacts the immune system. Research alsosuggests that sleep deprivation may lead to weight gain, high blood pressure, cancer, heart disease, stroke, diabetes, bone loss, and depression to name a few. According to Eve Van Cauter of the University of Chicago, a "lack of sleep disrupts every physiologic function in the body."[7]

Remember the saying *I will sleep when I am dead?* Well guess what, you sure will and much sooner than you should if you don't get enough sleep now!

2) Nutrition

Food is energy that converts to energy and you and I are what we eat and drink. There are tons of books on food, diet, and nutrition and I have read dozens of them. One of my recent favorites is *Perfect Health Diet* by Dr. Paul Jaminet,[8] and I'm also a big fan of Dr. Mark Hyman and Dr. Andrew Weil. I suggest studying the similarities in all these books.

The key is this: If food was made in a factory it is not real food. Unfortunately, our food supply has radically altered over time. Even the store produce we consume is not the same on the cellular level that it was decades ago. What is happening is scary stuff. Many big companies are more concerned about profit than the best quality nutrition.

---

[6] Dr. Bert Jacobson, professor and head of the School of Educational Studies at Oklahoma State University (OSU) says, "Sleep deprivation impacts us physically, which can negatively affect our coordination, agility, mood and energy. Research shows that sleep and athletics performance are related as sleeping better and longer leads to improvements in athletic performance, including faster sprint time, better endurance, lower heart rate, and even improved mood and higher levels of energy during a workout." Better Sleep Council, "Americans Get Physical After a Good Night in Bed," http://bettersleep.org/better-sleep/healthy-sleep/physical-performance-sleep.

[7] Rob Stein, "Scientists Finding Out What Losing Sleep Does to a Body," The Washington Post, October 9, 2005, http://www.washingtonpost.com/wp-dyn/content/article/2005/10/08/AR2005100801405.html

[8] Paul Jaminet and Shou-Ching Jaminet, Perfect Health Diet: Regain Health and Lose Weight by Eating the Way You Were Meant to Eat (New York: Scribner, 2013).

You should eat mostly vegetables with added lean protein. Healthy fats as well as balancing the gut are important strategies to follow. I also subscribe to schools of thought like Ayurveda that maintain the diet should match the individual and offer different recommendations based on specific body types.

In addition, you should consume at least two-thirds your body weight of clean water in ounces (if you weigh 180 pounds, you should drink at least 121 ounces of water a day).[9] And, you should drink more when you exercise and if you live in a warm climate.

3) Exercise

Chris Crowley's book *Younger Next Year* discusses the importance of cardio and weight training.[10] I also suggest adding core strength and flexibility into your repertoire like Ashtanga Yoga, my favorite.

The bottom line is that you need—yes, *need*—to invest time, money, and energy into a regular ongoing exercise program. At least six days a week.

There is so much evidence in relation to your own physical, mental, and emotional performance that you really cannot logically argue that you don't have the time. Find something you enjoy doing that agrees with your body and do it. Period.

4) Meditation

I encourage all my coaching clients to have a daily mediation practice. Many, who have followed my advice and created the habit, have said that the time they dedicate to meditation offers tremendous dividends.

The founder of Transcendental Meditation recommends meditating twice a day for twenty minutes. This forty-minute investment has significant impact on performance. In fact, this form of meditation

---

[9] Kristen Mccaffery, "How to Calculate How Much Water You Should Drink A Day," Slender Kitchen, September 14, 2012, http://nutrition-now.com/2009/06/water-how-much-do-you-need-to-drink/

[10] Chris Crowley and Henry S. Lodge, Younger Next Year: Live Strong, Fit, and Sexy—Until You're 80 and Beyond (New York: Workman Publishing Company, 2007)

is used by many famous people including the Beatles, Howard Stern, Jerry Seinfeld, Clint Eastwood, Mick Jagger, Deepak Chopra and others you would recognize.[11]

Meditation is kind of like exercise for our brains and many studies have shown that it helps with overall health and wellness, memory, stress relief, relaxation, and actually can change the brain's gray matter.[12]

I spent years studying meditation to discern what was common among all the practices. In essence there are two general types of meditation: one is where you sit and focus on a word, a mantra, the flow of your thoughts, your breath, or nothing at all; and the other type is mindfulness. This is a practice of staying focused on whatever you are doing and being in the moment with it.

A great example is mindful eating where you concentrate only on the process of eating and how the food is nourishing your body. Nothing else is on your mind at the time. Both of these types of meditations are worthwhile and should be integrated into your life.

Think of it this way: Your ability to direct your attention and focus is everything. Meditation is the place to sharpen this ability.

5) Gratitude

We already talked about the many benefits of gratitude in Chapter 2, but this simple adjustment in your life can help you change your paradigms and set your intentions in motion. Remember, gratitude is tied to the Law of Cause and Effect—the more you give thanks for something, the more it will come into your life.

There are many ways to practice gratitude. Try some of these simple ideas: send thank you letters, count your blessings throughout the day, mentally thank someone as you drive or commute to work, generate the good feelings that are associated with gratitude within yourself and then allow them to radiate outward when you meditate or pray, or keep a gratitude journal.

[11] Eco Warrior Chick, "Celebrities Who Practice Transcendental Meditation," Ranker.com, accessed March 11, 2016, http://www.ranker.com/list/celebrities-who-practice-transcendental-meditation/eco-warrior-chick.

[12] Lecia Bushak, "Meditation Changes the Brain's Very Structure—In a Good Way," *Medical Daily*, January 24, 2015, http://www.medicaldaily.com/mental-health-benefits-meditation-itll-alter-your-brains-grey-matter-and-improve-319298.

I use *The Five-Minute Journal* gratitude exercise with my clients.[13] At the beginning of the day, they write down three things that they are thankful for to set their intentions, and then at the end of the day, they write down what happened that they were grateful for. It helps them choose what to focus on throughout the day and helps generate more gratitude in their lives.

6) Renewal

One of my favorite stories from Stephen Covey, author of *The 7 Habits of Highly Effective People*, is that of the lumberjacks who were competing to cut down trees one day. Whoever could cut the most down would win. Each lumberjack had the same type of saw and started at the same time.

However one of the lumberjacks continued to leave and return. His competitors witnessed him coming and going and believed they would win the contest. At the end of the day the amount of wood was counted and the lumberjack who had left throughout the day won by quite a margin.

The loser blurted, "How can this be? You left several times throughout the day and I worked harder and longer then you, clearly I should be the winner!"

The winner smiled and explained that each time he left he did so to sharpen his saw.[14]

You, too, need to sharpen your saw. Daily, weekly, monthly, and yearly. Sleep, nutrition, exercise, meditation, and renewal are five strategies you can use on a daily basis.

I also suggest taking weekends off and taking vacations quarterly or biannually. I just came back from a two-week trip and am planning one for the fall and another for the following spring.

[13]Alex Ikonn and Uj Ramdas, The Five-Minute Journal (Intelligent Change, Inc., 2013). See also http://www.fiveminutejournal.com/.

[14] Stephen Covey, The 7 Habits of Highly Effective People: Powerful Lessons in Personal Change (New York: Free Press, 2004)

With discipline, health, and wellness
in your life, you will find excellence
and meet your potential. Without these,
your life will simply be mediocre.
You are better than that.

Going Deeper

- How are you sharpening your saw?
- What choices can you make to optimize your health and energy?

Chapter 7

Do You Have a Mentor?

Do not conform to the pattern of this world,
but be transformed by the renewing of your mind.
Then you will be able to test and approve what
God's will is—his good, pleasing and perfect will.[1]

---

[1] Romans 12:2.

The Power of a Coach or Mentor

In our own transformation, each of us needs to navigate through the various generations of development in our journey, yet we might not know how.

In this book we have discussed many of the elements required for you to become the best version of yourself so that you can truly align your soul with your life. It is imperative to understand that you are in control. You…yes *you* are the conduit to your vision.

The common denominator for all the clients
I have worked with is that they had
a level of clarity of what they wanted
to change in their lives, but couldn't
see the forest through the trees.

Let's face it, if you have a vision for a better personal and professional life why haven't you achieved it?

If you truly could get there on your own, wouldn't you be there already?

Create Success Without Struggle

There were many times in the last twelve years I wanted more and struggled to get there. I had a vision, I had goals, and I had drive. I worked harder than I ever had in my life. Yet the harder I beat my head against the wall, the more I got bruised.

I read every book I could get my hands on that covered some type of personal development. I attended seminars and I listened to ten to fifteen hours of personal development audios in my car every week. I experienced myself flowing with perspective and strategy and I felt I was acting in accordance. Yet, my outcomes failed to change.

The moment I hired a coach,
my life began to REALLY change.

My first coach and mentor was Tom Shields, who is an amazing and extremely insightful man. Tom provided me with a new perspective and was able to shine light in areas I simply had no way to see. Through our work together I began to notice changes—first internally, then externally. Tom helped me become conscious and aware at a level I didn't know was possible. He empowered me to plug into my source, which led to many breakthroughs.

Several times over the last eight years, I have worked with other mentors and consultants that had strengths and talents I wanted to leverage. In many cases I invested quite a bit of money to do this. Honestly, it was uncomfortable. I stretched myself. The financial obligation caused me to be deeply committed to doing whatever it took to get a return. The end result? Massive transformation.

Who Will Your Next Mentor Be?

Quite frankly, I know the challenge with hiring a coach or a consultant is that most of them are not very good at getting their clients to a place of permanent change. Many of them are not living what they say and teach. They focus on what to do, not *how* to do it. And they certainly don't ask you *why* you want to do it.

> ### *In order to alter behavior we need to understand why the behavior exists and how it serves us today.*

We need to be able to map out specifically how things must change so that we can arrive at our preferred outcome. Eric Hoffer says, "In times of change, learners inherit the earth, while the learned find themselves beautifully equipped to deal with a world that no longer exists."[2]

Who do you want to be?

The ability to lead another person on a journey of personal discovery and transformation not only requires skill but also intuition. It is the goal we all seek.

Before we part ways I want to ask you one last question: Are you fulfilled, happy, at peace, and living an ideal life?

If not, let's talk.

You have one life. *Make it count.*

---

[2] To read more quotes from Eric Hoffer, see https://www.goodreads.com/author/quotes/9843. Eric_Hoffer.

Interested in *Going Deeper?*

Email me at chris@chrisyonker.com

www.chrisyonker.com

About the Author

Chris Yonker is a leading consultant to Fortune 100 companies, entrepreneurs, celebrities, and top sales professionals, and offers next-level business strategy coaching for every type of personal and professional ambition. As an Executive Performance Coach, Chris uses powerful tools from various teaching practices, including leadership principles, martial arts, spiritual awareness, and neuro-linguistic programming (NLP) to help restore work-life balance and inner harmony so you can plug back into your own orbit and achieve an even higher level. He is married and lives in the Seacoast Region with his wife, Jolie.

Made in the USA
Columbia, SC
17 August 2018